6 Decisions

That Will Change Your Life

6 Decisions
That Will Change Your Life

Participant Workbook
DVD
Leader Guide

6 Things
We Should Know About God

Participant Workbook
DVD
Leader Guide

6 Ways
We Encounter God

Participant Workbook
DVD
Leader Guide

6 Decisions

That Will Change Your Life

Participant Workbook

Tom Berlin

with Justin Lucas

Abingdon Press
Nashville

Six Decisions That Will Change Your Life
Participant Workbook

Tom Berlin with Justin Lucas

Copyright © 2014 by Abingdon Press
All rights reserved.

This book is printed on acid-free, elemental chlorine-free paper.

ISBN 978-1-426-79444-5

14 15 16 17 18 19 20 21 22 23—10 9 8 7 6 5 4 3 2 1
MANUFACTURED IN THE UNITED STATES OF AMERICA

With God's help, I will draw closer to Christ through this six-week study as I commit to read the Bible and prayerfully reflect on its meaning for my life.

_____

My Name

_____

Start Date

Contents

Welcome!

We're glad you are participating in *Six Decisions That Will Change Your Life*. When you commit yourself to this six-week journey, we believe you will grow deeper in your relationship with Christ. You will gain the most from this study if you make the following practices a part of your journey:

1. **Attend a small group.** Your church offers small group opportunities where spiritual transformation can be encouraged and enhanced through community. Those gathered will have the opportunity to share and discuss their insights, questions, and life experiences and, most importantly, to apply lessons learned about their personal and corporate study. The study includes, in addition to this Participant Workbook, a DVD and Leader Guide to enhance learning and group involvement. We encourage all to join a small group for this study.

2. **Use the Participant Workbook five days a week.** This book is intended to draw you into a daily conversation with God by guiding you in reading key Scripture passages, responding to reflective questions, and journaling your thoughts about how this encounter applies to your life.

3. **Attend worship.** Our conversation with God is incomplete if we don't participate in individual and corporate worship. Go to church every week, but during the study make a special point of attending.

How to Use This Book

When you use this book each day, begin your time with prayer. Read the Bible passages assigned for the day. Answer the questions provided, journal on your own, or do a combination of these two options.

Write out a Scripture verse that speaks to you from the assigned reading. It may be a verse of encouragement, instruction, confession, or insight.

Observe what the verse says, and write a few sentences about its relevance to your life.

Relate the text to your life by applying it to a specific issue you are considering, a problem you are facing, or an encouragement God wants you to hear. Write a short paragraph in which you share what you are hearing from God's Word.

Decide to share with God the desire of your heart. As a result of reading this text, what do you want to do and who do you want to become? Share your thoughts by writing a short prayer to conclude your conversation with God.

Week One

The Decision to Follow

Day
1

Key Verse

Then Nathanael declared, "Rabbi, you are the Son of God; you are the king of Israel."

John 1:49 NIV

1. Why were John the Baptist's disciples willing to change rabbis and follow Jesus so suddenly?

_____

_____

_____

2. Andrew brought Simon to Jesus. Philip told Nathanael. Who was instrumental in bringing you to Christ, and how did they influence you?

Faith in Action

Discipline yourself to do the Bible readings and journal in this book every day.

_____

_____

_____

_____

_____

Going Deeper

Many people are trying to understand their purpose in life. We hope that God will speak to us in some way. The men listed in John 1 got an invitation from Jesus himself to join him on a journey. While they did not know Jesus' identity at this point, they heard John the Baptist call Jesus the Lamb of God. The phrase must have reminded them of the lamb that was slain when the Israelites were escaping from slavery in Egypt. To ensure that the angel of death would "pass over" their homes during the plague of the firstborn, they were to sacrifice a lamb without any blemish and place a mark of its blood over the doorway. John was telling people something significant about Jesus that no one would have been able to comprehend at that time. These men did understand that important things were going to happen with Jesus.

This was an important decision for two of John's disciples. Switching rabbis was equivalent to changing universities in your junior year of college. Rabbis were Jewish teachers who had been given the authority to interpret the Scriptures so that people knew how to live a holy life. A disciple had to be chosen by his rabbi and agree to submit completely to his rabbi's interpretation of the Scripture. By switching rabbis from John to Jesus, the disciples were leaving their old interpretation of Scripture behind and promising to believe Jesus' interpretation fully. Jesus calls us to follow him as well. Just as the first disciples' lives were changed when they made a decision to follow Jesus, so our lives will be changed as well.

Notable Quotable

"He is no fool who gives what he cannot keep to gain that which he cannot lose."
—Jim Elliot

Going Deeper Questions

3. When you think of Jesus as "the Lamb of God," what does that mean to you?

_____

_____

_____

_____

_____

4. What is the hardest thing you've had to give up in following Christ? Is there anything you are called to give up now?

_____

_____

_____

_____

_____

Today's Scripture

Exodus 3:1–4:17

Key Verse

God said to Moses, "I AM WHO I AM." And he said, "Say this to the people of Israel, 'I AM has sent me to you.'"

Exodus 3:14 ESV

1. Why can't Moses set foot on the ground around the burning bush with shoes on?

_____

_____

_____

_____

2. Moses comes up with lots of excuses for why he shouldn't follow God's call for him. What excuses have kept you from following where God calls you?

_____

_____

_____

_____

Going Deeper

For many people, the thought of directly hearing the voice of God telling them what to do would be a dream come true and the answer to their most heartfelt prayers. Moses, however, finds that it is not so easy. He is fearful of following the voice of God because sometimes God asks us to do things that we don't understand, things that we aren't ready for.

When Moses first approaches the burning bush, God's voice tells him to take off his shoes. It seems like an odd request, but consider friends who ask you to take off your shoes before you come inside their home. You may comply to keep their carpet clean, but it is also a sign of respecting their authority—their house, their rules. By having Moses remove his shoes, God was claiming authority over everything—nature, the Israelites, Moses, everything.

Moses yields his rights to God's authority, but he is still overwhelmed by God's direction. He comes up with many excuses to avoid his role in the plan God shares—"I'm not important enough." "I'm not a good enough follower." "No one will listen to me." "I don't speak very well." "I really don't want to go!" For every excuse Moses makes, God has an answer. Sometimes we find it hard to follow because God has more confidence in us and our abilities than we have in ourselves. Other times it is hard to follow because the task we are undertaking is difficult or because we feel unworthy of being asked by a holy God to do anything. The good news is that God uses ordinary people to bless others, and sometimes they do extraordinary things.

> ### Notable Quotable
>
> *"Being a Christian is more than just an instantaneous conversion. It is a daily process whereby you grow to be more and more like Christ."*
> —Billy Graham

Going Deeper Questions

3. In what area of your life do you find it hardest to yield to God's authority? Why?

_____

_____

_____

_____

_____

4. God calls each of us to step out in faith, sometimes in small ways and sometimes in big ways. What do you feel called to do, and how can you accept that calling?

_____

_____

_____

_____

_____

Today's Scripture

Judges 4

Key Verse

Then Barak said to her, "If you will go with me, then I will go; but if you will not go with me, I will not go."

Judges 4:8 NASB

1. What opportunities are lost when we ignore God's call?

_____

_____

_____

_____

_____

2. Barak refuses to fight against Sisera until Deborah joins his quest. What struggles do you face that could be easier if you asked friends to come to your aid? Who would you ask for help?

_____

_____

_____

_____

_____

Going Deeper

Just like Moses, Barak hears a clear commandment of God through Deborah, one of the great judges of Israel. He experiences fear at this request, knowing that he is being sent into battle against a formidable enemy. Following will mean great sacrifice and even death. There is also a cost, however, for not following. The security of the nation is at stake, and it is the role of the general to face that challenge.

While you may not be facing an enemy army, no doubt there are people in your life who depend on you. There are service projects to do, church functions to attend, friends who may never hear the gospel unless you share it with them—not to mention schoolwork, housework, homework, yardwork, paperwork, and busy work. Sometimes it just doesn't feel like you can make it on your own, but maybe that's OK. One of the wise things that Barak does is invite Deborah to accompany him. He seems not to care that this will have the appearance of cowardice or that a woman will gain a great reputation when the opposing general is defeated. In order to follow, Barak knows that he needs a companion and an ally in his corner.

Notable Quotable

"It is a great deal easier to do that which God gives us to do, no matter how hard it is, than to face the responsibilities of not doing it."
—J. R. Miller

Like Barak, we often find ourselves outnumbered by the stresses of life and the magnitude of what we are called to accomplish. We all need a community of fellow believers around us, friends who can help us in the tough times and push us to greater things in the good times. We need to be able to share our lives and our struggles, to "bear each other's burdens," and to keep each other strong. And the best way to do that is to be a burden-carrier for others.

Going Deeper Questions

3. Where have you found friends who have bolstered your courage and made it easier for you to follow God's call? How can you thank them for their fellowship?

_____

_____

_____

_____

_____

4. What is one area of your life where you feel called to follow God but are struggling to do so? How could you share that burden with a friend?

_____

_____

_____

_____

_____

Day 4

Today's Scripture
Luke 3:1-18

Key Verse

John answered them all, saying, "I baptize you with water, but he who is mightier than I is coming, the strap of whose sandals I am not worthy to untie. He will baptize you with the Holy Spirit and fire."

Luke 3:16 ESV

1. John preached "a baptism of repentance." Why are visible actions an important part of following Christ's call?

_____

_____

_____

_____

2. When questioned, John gives specific actions that people can do to enact God's will in their lives. What actions can you take to make Christ's love apparent in your life?

_____

_____

_____

_____

Going Deeper

Sometimes we can hear the voice of God through simple words that challenge us to obedience. We read the Bible, listen to a sermon, or hear the advice of a trusted friend, and we realize that something in our life is not as it should be.

John the Baptist's preaching left people with an important question: what should I do? They felt convicted and wanted to repent of their sins. The word "conviction" has two meanings: "a firmly held belief" and "a formal declaration that someone is guilty of an offense." In Christianity, the word takes on both meanings simultaneously. We are all convicted sinners. We have been declared guilty and deserve punishment for our guilt. In this conviction comes the opportunity for pardon. We are given the option to repent, to turn away fully from the mistakes we've made and run in the other direction, back inside the gracious boundaries of obedience to God.

> **Notable Quotable**
>
> *"In this life we cannot do great things. We can only do small things with big love."*
>
> —Mother Teresa of Calcutta

Conviction is one way that God speaks to us. Change comes only when we admit our shortcomings and ask God for help. Our desire to turn in God's direction and be obedient is how we respond to that conviction. John was more than happy to point out the obvious changes that his listeners needed to make: don't extort money, don't collect more than you should, share with the poor. These are obvious changes, and the decision to make them is life-changing.

Going Deeper Questions

3. What actions in your life do you feel most convicted about? Have you fully admitted your guilt, or do you still make excuses about those actions?

_____

_____

_____

_____

_____

_____

4. What are some obvious steps of obedience you can make in the areas of life where you feel convicted?

_____

_____

_____

_____

_____

_____

Day 5

Today's Scripture
1 John 5:1-12

Key Verse

By this we know that we love the children of God, when we love God and keep His commandments.

1 John 5:2 NKJV

1. What does our obedience have to do with how we love God?

_____

_____

_____

_____

_____

2. In other venues of your life (sports teams, community organizations, schools, and so on), following the rules is necessary to be part of the group. Why, then, is it so hard to do this when it comes to being Christian?

_____

_____

_____

_____

_____

Going Deeper

The book of 1 John makes a compelling case regarding the importance of following Jesus Christ as a way of hearing the will of God for your life. At the time 1 John was written, a splinter group of Christians had broken off and were teaching that Jesus was so divine that he had no humanity. The author of 1 John wanted people to know that in Jesus, God had come as a man who lived in ordinary circumstances. Christ was divine, but he was also fully human and understood the complexities of human existence completely as one who experienced it fully. This was a revolutionary idea, that God would come in human form and guide us in the way we live our lives. No longer could people say that God did not understand what it was like to face the difficulties of being a human. First John states repeatedly that to be a Christian, one must confess that Jesus Christ has come in flesh.

> ### Notable Quotable
>
> *"To say that I am made in the image of God is to say that love is the reason for my existence, for God is love. Love is my true identity. Selflessness is my true self. Love is my true character. Love is my name."*
> —Thomas Merton

As a wise person once said, the importance of any journey is where it takes you in the end. First John tells us that Christ has the ability not only to guide our steps in this life but also to take us to eternal life as well. He was not just "a good teacher" but the creator of all things, not just a man God used but God in human form. He came not to give "secret" knowledge of how God works to a chosen few but to open the path to salvation to everyone throughout eternity.

First John calls its readers to demonstrate the love of Christ in the church and in the world. This happens when our experience of Christ's love leaves us with a desire to be obedient to him in the decisions we make and the callings we pursue.

Going Deeper Questions

3. Why is it important that Jesus is both God and man? What does that mean to you?

_____

_____

_____

_____

_____

4. How can we use our love for God and for others to help prove to the world that Jesus is the only way to true life?

_____

_____

_____

_____

_____

The Decision
for a New Life

Today's Scripture

John 3

Key Verse

But those who do what is true come to the light, so that it may be clearly seen that their deeds have been done in God.

John 3:21 NRSV

1. Why did Nicodemus find the term "born again" confusing?

_____

_____

_____

_____

_____

2. What does it mean to be "born again"?

_____

_____

_____

_____

_____

_____

Faith in Action

Prayer is one of the most important spiritual disciplines to practice. Each day this week, set aside 10 minutes to pray for your life and for people you know who need to experience God's gift of new life.

Going Deeper

Following a path often leads to places of decision, where the path forks left and right. Taking one direction or pursuing the other will have real consequences. Nicodemus was a rabbi, which meant he was both a teacher and a spiritual leader. The rabbis were the most educated members of Hebrew society, men who had memorized the Scriptures in totality and were the only ones allowed to interpret those Scriptures for the people. As a member of the Jewish Council, he was highly esteemed as a man of both spiritual and political clout. This was a man with considerable power in Jesus' era. However, he was also an intellectually honest man who was willing to consider how Jesus was interpreting the Scriptures. Because he was open to learning more about God, Nicodemus experienced Jesus' ministry as a fork in the road. He truly longed to understand what Jesus was teaching, especially what he meant by the phrase "you must be born from above."

In his explanation, Jesus makes a powerful statement that most Christians have committed to memory—John 3:16: "For God so loved the world that he gave his only Son, so that everyone who believes in him may not perish but may have eternal life." Many writers have claimed that this single statement encapsulates the whole purpose of Jesus and God's offer of salvation, and it is easy to see why. Here, Jesus claims that he is the Son of God who came to save the world, not only from death but from eternal separation from God. He explains that God's overflowing love is at the root of this salvation and that our starting point is to believe in that love and follow Jesus' example in his love for God and others. That's what it means to be born again: to give up the darkness of the world around us and to enter into the light of new life.

Notable Quotable

"It may be hard for an egg to turn into a bird: it would be a jolly sight harder for it to learn to fly while remaining an egg. We are like eggs at present. And you cannot go on indefinitely being just an ordinary, decent egg. We must be hatched or go bad."
—C. S. Lewis

31

Going Deeper Questions

3. What would you be willing to give up for God's will? Why is the imagery of God giving up the only Son so powerful?

_____

_____

_____

_____

_____

_____

4. Why is new life such an important part of being a Christian? How would you describe the experience to others?

_____

_____

_____

_____

_____

_____

Day 2

Key Verse

Now then, please swear to me by the LORD that you will show kindness to my family, because I have shown kindness to you.

Joshua 2:12 NIV

1. Why do you think Rahab hid the Israelite spies when it could have caused serious problems for her?

_____

_____

_____

_____

_____

2. Why do you think God chose Rahab, a Gentile prostitute, to help the Israelites and become a part of Jesus' genealogy?

_____

_____

_____

_____

_____

Going Deeper

Sometimes a decision we make to do God's will changes everything. By harboring the spies of Israel, Rahab knew that she was severing her ties with the people of Jericho. That's not to say that her life in Jericho was glamorous. Rahab was a harlot, or prostitute, which means she would have rented out her rooms to lustful men of Jericho as well as to men visiting town from foreign lands. In that time period, a woman who was unmarried and had no male family members to defend and care for her would often turn to prostitution because it was one of the very few ways that she could make an income. But this would have put her at the lowest end of society, a person without friends, ignored by all but the men who misused her.

The Israelite spies probably chose to stay at Rahab's house because it was not unusual for her to house outsiders. It is possible that Rahab was drawn to the God of her Hebrew guests because they told her the truth and did not take advantage of her. She took the bold step of hiding the spies, asking in return that they rescue her when the Israelites fought against Jericho.

> ## Notable Quotable
>
> *"We are not the sum of our weaknesses and failures; we are the sum of the Father's love for us and our real capacity to become the image of his Son."*
>
> —Pope John Paul II

When Joshua later besieged the city, Rahab and her household were spared. She gave herself over to the Hebrew God and became a part of the people of Israel, beginning a new life. That decision led to greater things than she could imagine. She married an Israelite named Salmon, and together they had a son named Boaz, who would become the great-grandfather of King David. And in David's bloodline was born the greatest king of all, Jesus Christ. Rahab's decision to leave her old life changed more than her own story. It changed the world.

Going Deeper Questions

3. Where in your life have you seen the hand of God at work? What changes have you seen as a result?

_____

_____

_____

_____

_____

4. What small things has God asked you to do that could change the world around you for the better?

_____

_____

_____

_____

_____

Today's Scripture
Ezekiel 37:1-14

Key Verse

Therefore, prophesy and say to them: This is what the Lord GOD says: I am going to open your graves and bring you up from them, My people, and lead you into the land of Israel.

Ezekiel 37:12 HCSB

1. What did Ezekiel's vision mean to the nation of Israel at that time? What might it mean for us today?

_____

_____

_____

_____

_____

2. Has God ever called you to do something you thought was impossible? Write it down and explain how God helped you through that situation.

_____

_____

_____

_____

_____

Going Deeper

Ezekiel was a prophet at a very dark time in Israel's history. Israel had broken into two countries, Israel and Judah, with two different kings. Both countries fell into idol worship, and God punished them by allowing the surrounding nations to conquer them. First, the Assyrians destroyed the country of Israel in 722 B.C., then the Babylonians came in and took over the whole area in 586 B.C., exiling most of the Israelites from the Promised Land.

Ezekiel was one of those swept up in the Babylonian Exile after Judah had tried—and failed—to rebel against Babylon. He did not hold a grudge against the Babylonians for destroying his people. Ezekiel placed the blame squarely on the people of Judah for turning their backs on God's commandments. That's why, in this vision, he compares Israel to a pile of dry, old bones lying in a desolate valley. God speaks a word of hope to Ezekiel that we find in this vision. God wants to raise the nation of Israel from the dead and give them new life if they will only turn back and follow God's commands.

> ## Notable Quotable
>
> *"Christ made my soul beautiful with the jewels of grace and virtue. I belong to him whom the angels serve."*
>
> —*St. Agnes*

Sometimes our lives feel like dry bones as well. We wonder if anything has the power to change us. Maybe a new diet, a new organizational plan, a new job, or a new relationship will bring new life. Ezekiel understood that there are some things that only God has the power to provide. For Israel to have new life, a future with hope, the fresh wind of God's Spirit would have to blow across their lives and circumstances and bring something new. The question to us is the same as to the prophet: do we believe that God has the power to bring new life?

Going Deeper Questions

3. Have you ever faced negative consequences when you failed to follow God's commands? Looking back, how can you see that as God trying to get your attention?

_____

_____

_____

_____

_____

4. What changes can you make to bring yourself out of exile and get a fresh wind of God's spirit in your life?

_____

_____

_____

_____

_____

Day 4

Today's Scripture
Luke 19:1-10; Psalm 32

Key Verse

I acknowledged my sin to You, And my iniquity I did not hide; I said, "I will confess my transgressions to the LORD"; and You forgave the guilt of my sin.

Psalm 32:5 NASB

1. Why was it surprising that Jesus wanted to go to Zacchaeus's house?

_____

_____

_____

_____

_____

2. What is the biggest thing you've ever given up for others? How did you grow from that experience?

_____

_____

_____

_____

_____

Going Deeper

Zacchaeus was possibly the most despised member of his community. He was a chief tax collector, which meant he worked for the Roman government taking money from the people Rome conquered—in this case, Zacchaeus's own people, the Israelites. The Romans allowed tax collectors to charge people as much as they wanted, as long as Rome got its share. As you can imagine, this didn't make Zacchaeus many friends. On one hand, Zacchaeus had everything wealth could buy. On the other hand, he had nothing at all. If ever a man had a good reason to seek a new life, it was Zacchaeus. The problem is that to find that life, he had to lose the life he had built.

Jesus had such an impact on Zacchaeus that by the end of their meal, the tax collector had made a decision for a new life. He offered to give back all he had taken from others and more. What a powerful moment it must have been when Jesus proclaimed in verse 9, "Today salvation has come to this house."

We often get into patterns of life that we have not examined. These patterns are unhealthy for us, or they may lead to a life that we don't really want to have. It's like eating junk food. It tastes good going down, but when you look back over time, you find that you're left feeling unhealthy and unsettled. God's will is to give us a life of meaning and joy. God wants to give us a life that is vibrant and growing deeper in our trust of Christ. Jesus always met people where they were, like he did with Zacchaeus, so that he could take them where God wanted them to be. Christ can bring salvation to any home, if we follow the example of Zacchaeus and welcome him inside.

> ## Notable Quotable
>
> *"Though I am not what I ought to be, nor what I wish to be, nor what I hope to be, I can truly say, I am not what I once was; and. . . by the grace of God, I am what I am!"*
>
> —John Newton, former slave trader, writer of the hymn "Amazing Grace"

Going Deeper Questions

3. In what ways has salvation come to your house? In what ways has God changed your life for the better?

_____

_____

_____

_____

_____

4. What patterns in your life are acting like spiritual junk food? What healthy patterns can you put in place to grow instead?

_____

_____

_____

_____

_____

Today's Scripture

Acts 2

Key Verse

Peter said to them, "Repent, and be baptized every one of you in the name of Jesus Christ so that your sins may be forgiven; and you will receive the gift of the Holy Spirit."

Acts 2:38 NRSV

1. In what ways is Peter different in this chapter than he is at other times in the Bible?

_____

_____

_____

_____

_____

2. How does your life and your church resemble the ideal church described in Acts 2? How can you make them more alike?

_____

_____

_____

_____

_____

Going Deeper

When we make decisions to live a new life, God can really change us. Think about how Peter changed during his time with Christ. He started out as a fisherman, and when Jesus gave him a miraculous catch of fish, Peter fell to his knees and begged Jesus to go away because he felt too sinful to have Jesus around. By the time Jesus walked on water, Peter had grown in courage enough to step out on the water and join in Jesus' miracle. But when he got out of the boat, Peter got scared and started to sink before he could reach

Notable Quotable

"The gospel life isn't something we learn about and then put together with instructions from the manufacturer; it's something we become as God does his work of creation and salvation in us and as we accustom ourselves to a life of belief and obedience and prayer."

—Eugene Peterson

Jesus. This same Peter, who once boasted of his loyalty to Christ, ran away when Jesus was arrested and lied about ever knowing the Lord.

Peter is the perfect example of how imperfect we can be sometimes as Christians. But God still chooses to use us if we will make ourselves available. In this reading, after Christ's crucifixion and resurrection, Peter, filled with the Holy Spirit, speaks openly of his faith to a crowd of thousands. His willingness to openly share the good news of Jesus' life, death, and resurrection was the evidence of his transformation. God's Spirit fell on this crowd and used Peter's words to bring many to follow Christ. They formed the first expression of the early church, sharing all things in common. The love of that community was evidence that their lives were new. These first followers discovered something important in their life together. It is not enough to find new life; you must sustain it as well. This is why they met together regularly: to worship God, to encourage each other, and to enjoy the fellowship of others who saw life differently from the larger society in which they lived. New life was very important for Peter and the early church, but it was only the beginning. They chose to grow together, and from that personal growth came a growth in numbers and influence in their community.

Going Deeper Questions

3. Why do you think God uses broken, imperfect people to share the perfect gift of the Gospel?

_____

_____

_____

_____

_____

4. What changes in your life could make you a more effective witness for Christ?

_____

_____

_____

_____

_____

*The Decision
to Mature*

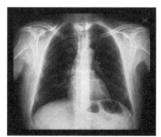

Day 1

Today's Scripture
John 4

Key Verse

They said to the woman, "We no longer believe just because of what you said; now we have heard for ourselves, and we know that this man really is the Savior of the world."

John 4:42 NIV

1. What did the Samaritan woman already know (or think she knew) about the Messiah?

_____

_____

_____

_____

_____

Faith in Action

To hear God's still, small voice, we need to practice listening. This week, spend 10 minutes per day in silence thinking about how God wants you to mature in your Christian walk.

2. Why do we sometimes refuse to learn new or hard things about Jesus? How can we overcome that reticence?

_____

_____

_____

_____

Going Deeper

Speaking to a Samaritan woman was a very unusual act for a Jewish rabbi like Jesus. For one thing, the Israelites and the Samaritans were not exactly on good terms with one another. When the Assyrians conquered Israel, some of the Israelites from the region of Samaria intermarried with the Assyrians as a way of keeping their families safe. They also began worshiping the Assyrian gods and intertwined that worship with their Jewish belief system. Marrying non-Israelites and worshiping other gods were strictly prohibited by Mosaic law, so these Samaritans were much despised by the Hebrews.

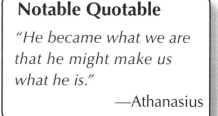

Notable Quotable

"He became what we are that he might make us what he is."

—Athanasius

Hebrew men also did not talk to unknown women in public. If the woman was married, it could be said that the woman was pursuing another man, and by the laws of the day, her husband could divorce her over it. If she was unmarried, and coming in the middle of the day, it could mean that she was somehow unclean, a person who wanted to avoid the crowds who would gather at the well in the morning.

Jesus had many reasons not to speak to her . . . but he did, and she listened to him. This woman believed in the prospect of a Messiah. However, it was a far greater step of faith to believe that Jesus was *the* Messiah. Her decision to take this step of maturity in her faith in God arose from a deep spiritual thirst that Jesus understood. This thirst seemed to be impacting her relational and moral decisions. Jesus' compassion to this woman is the one he demonstrates to us today. It is the reason that all of us can be humble as we come to know him and joyful that he wants to offer us the living water of his grace.

Going Deeper Questions

3. Sometimes it is hard to come to Jesus when we are hurting. How does Jesus meet the Samaritan woman where she is on her spiritual journey?

_____

_____

_____

_____

_____

_____

4. What "secret" struggle keeps you from giving your life to God completely? How can you accept the living water to wash that sin away?

_____

_____

_____

_____

_____

_____

Day 2

Today's Scripture

Judges 6

Key Verse

The LORD turned to him and said, "Go in the strength you have and deliver Israel from the power of Midian. Am I not sending you?"

Judges 6:14 HCSB

1. Why did Gideon test God, and how did God respond?

_____

_____

_____

_____

_____

_____

2. What things in your life cause you to hesitate in following God?

_____

_____

_____

_____

_____

_____

Going Deeper

Taking steps toward a more mature faith almost always entails taking a risk. Gideon was working inside a wine press because he did not want to take the risk of being seen by the Midianites. A wine press, which was fully enclosed, would have been a terrible location for threshing wheat, which requires a large space and wind to separate the wheat kernels from the chaff. Gideon was unwilling to even thresh wheat openly, but God asked him to take a far greater risk, to lead men in battle and bring security to Israel.

At first, it seems like Gideon responds to the call pretty well, immediately offering a sacrifice before the angel of the Lord. But God wasn't asking Gideon for an animal sacrifice. God was asking Gideon to give up his time, his efforts, and his plans in order to bring peace and security to the Israelites. Like most of us, Gideon wanted a sign or two to confirm that this was what God wanted him to do

> **Notable Quotable**
>
> *"If we cannot believe God when our circumstances appear to be against us, we do not believe Him at all."*
> —Charles Spurgeon

before taking a risk. Wouldn't it be great if God gave each of us such strong encouragements for our decisions?

By the end of his story, Gideon would have to take many steps toward a more mature faith. He would have to learn how to follow God's will without getting sign after sign to confirm his judgment. Gideon would have to trust that God could take what little faith he had and lead him to be one of the greatest generals of Israel. Once he learned to follow God intuitively, he was used in ways that blessed not only himself but Israel as a whole. When we learn to trust God in the small things, it often leads to places where we become involved in the most significant and meaningful work of our lives.

Going Deeper Questions

3. Did Gideon really want a sign or was he trying to complicate things so God wouldn't use him? Have you ever done something like that?

_____

_____

_____

_____

_____

_____

4. What sign will it take for you to allow your relationship with God to mature?

_____

_____

_____

_____

_____

_____

Today's Scripture
Luke 15:11-32

Key Verse

"For this son of mine was dead and is alive again; he was lost and is found." So they began to celebrate.

Luke 15:24 NIV

1. How does the prodigal son change throughout this story? Does the father change at all?

_____

_____

_____

_____

_____

2. Is there any part of your life that you have refused to change for God?

_____

_____

_____

_____

_____

Going Deeper

The parable of the prodigal son is sometimes called the parable of the loving father, because the focus of Jesus' teaching is on the consistency of God's love for us. Our focus, however, is on the maturity that came to the prodigal son that is captured in the phrase "when he came to his senses." Sometimes maturity of faith arises out of the pain we experience in life. Going our own way may lead to unintended consequences that damage our relationships, squander our resources, and neglect our love of others. One excellent example of this comes from the ancient Christian bishop Augustine of Hippo. As a young man, Augustine was raised by his Christian mother, but he left home and avoided the church for many years. He led a hedonistic life, found girlfriends and a mistress, and pursued pleasure and wealth. He lived by the saying, "Lord, grant me chastity and continence, but not yet!" (*Confessions*, Book 8).

> ### Notable Quotable
>
> *"Let us understand that God is a physician, and that suffering is a medicine for salvation, not a punishment for damnation."*
>
> —St. Augustine

Yet through it all, his mother prayed for him to return to the church. One day, Augustine was reading Paul's letter to the Romans, and was shaken by Romans 13:13-14, closing with "clothe yourselves with the Lord Jesus Christ, and do not think about how to gratify the desires of the flesh." He felt that God was calling him to radically change his life, so he swiftly did. He quit his job, left his mistress, sold his possessions, and became one of the greatest leaders of the early church. Rather than seeing a godly life as a place of restriction or punishment, Augustine realized that the Christian life provided him with gracious limits in which he found greater contentment and joy. He realized that the life he had was not as good as the life God could give him. This is what happened to the prodigal son. What a joy to know that his loving father was still waiting for him to return!

Going Deeper Questions

3. It has been said that we learn more from failure than success. List some things in your life that God has taught you through mistakes and trials.

_____

_____

_____

_____

_____

4. Have you ever had an "Aha!" moment when you knew that something in your life needed to change? What was it, and how have you changed since that realization?

_____

_____

_____

_____

_____

Day 4

Today's Scripture

Acts 10

Key Verse

Then Peter began to speak: "I now realize how true it is that God does not show favoritism but accepts from every nation the one who fears him and does what is right."

Acts 10:34-35 NIV

1. Why wouldn't Peter eat the animals God provided? How did God use this to teach him about God's love for the Gentiles?

_____

_____

_____

_____

_____

2. What are some examples, elsewhere in the Bible or in your own life, of God using unusual circumstances to teach God's followers how to live?

_____

_____

_____

_____

_____

Going Deeper

One of the greatest conflicts in the early church was whether the first followers of Jesus, who were all devout Jews and believed Jesus to be the Messiah and fulfillment of Judaism, could accept Gentiles—people who were not Jewish—into the church. Everything in their background taught them that no person could come to God without following the Torah, the Law of God found in the first five books of the Hebrew Bible.

This was far more than an intellectual question to resolve. It was a personally-held bitterness toward Gentiles, who had conquered and reconquered them throughout the centuries. At the time of Acts, the Jews were again under foreign occupation—this time by the Romans. Needless to say, it was difficult for the early Christians to forgive the Gentiles for the generations of warfare and servitude they had wrought. There was also an intense disgust toward the diet of Gentiles, which included pork and shellfish, items that were forbidden to Jews under the Law.

Centuries earlier, prophets had said that Israel would be a "light for the Gentiles" (Isaiah 49:6). Now the Holy Spirit was telling Peter that he would be instrumental in shining that light. This would be a series of decisions that slowly taught Peter to put his trust in God rather than his own instincts, experiences, and prejudices. It was a long process, sometimes marked with failures, but it was a necessary one for Peter and others. Steps of maturity often take us out of an old way of living, even one that has served us well, into a new way of life that has a deeper devotion to God.

> ### Notable Quotable
>
> *"When I was young, I was sure of everything; in a few years, having been mistaken a thousand times, I was not half so sure of most things as I was before; at present I am hardly sure of anything but what God has revealed to man.""*
>
> — John Wesley

Going Deeper Questions

3. What prejudices do you carry with you? Where do they come from, and how can you fix them?

_____

_____

_____

_____

_____

4. Who do you find it most difficult to reach out to in love? How does God want you to change your attitude?

_____

_____

_____

_____

_____

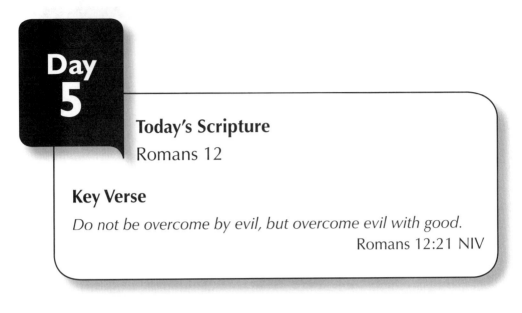

Day 5

Today's Scripture
Romans 12

Key Verse

Do not be overcome by evil, but overcome evil with good.
Romans 12:21 NIV

1. What does it mean to be "transformed by the renewing of your mind" in verse 2?

_____

_____

_____

_____

_____

2. Reread verses 9-21. Which things on this list come easily to you? Which ones are the most difficult?

_____

_____

_____

_____

_____

Going Deeper

In another letter, Paul called Christians to move from spiritual milk to solid food. Paul wanted people to be born anew in Christ, but he also wanted them to grow up and become Christian adults who had the ability to make decisions informed by their devotion to Christ.

C. S. Lewis was raised in a Christian home, but early in life, he decided to become an atheist. This was related to his mother's death, a moment that made him "very angry with God for not existing" (*Surprised by Joy,* p. 115). For many years, he struggled with a feeling that there must be a God controlling the universe, but intellectually, he couldn't wrap his mind around the truth. Through the patient prodding of Christian friends and the reading of Christian writers like G. K. Chesterton, Lewis found his way back to Christ—first to a belief that there was a God, and later, to God as Christ. Lewis learned to love God, see the wisdom and logic of joyfully following Christ, and share his faith with others.

> **Notable Quotable**
>
> *"Until you have given up your self to Him you will not have a real self."*
> —C. S. Lewis

In Romans 12, Paul gives us a list of ways we can allow God to change us and deepen our faith, as well as things to avoid if our goal is to honor God with our lives. One of the important aspects of maturing in the Christian faith is to become more obedient to Christ without becoming legalistic in our approach to discipleship. Legalism can lead to keeping the rules without a deeper love of God or other people. One hallmark of a mature faith is our ability to honor the commandments of God in a way that invites others to join us because of the joy and love found there.

Going Deeper Questions

3. What areas of Christianity make you question God? With what friends can you discuss these issues so that you can all grow in your knowledge of Christ?

_____

_____

_____

_____

_____

4. Where do you find yourself being most "rule-bound" and legalistic? In what ways do you feel led to change?

_____

_____

_____

_____

_____

The Decision to Respond

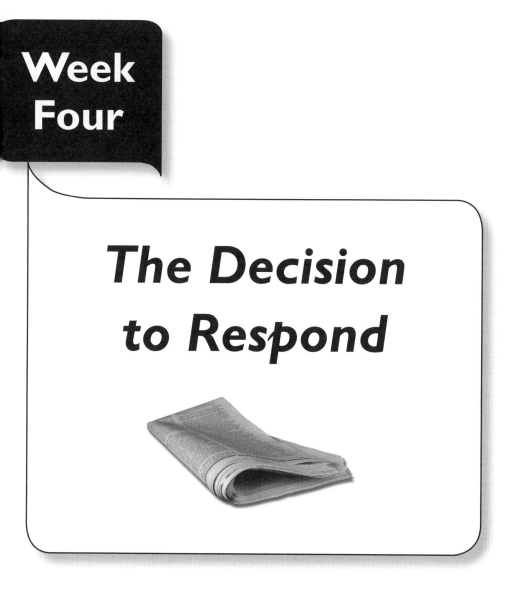

Day 1

Today's Scripture

John 6

Key Verse

"For this is the will of my Father, that everyone who looks on the Son and believes in him should have eternal life, and I will raise him up on the last day."

John 6:40 ESV

1. How do you compare the response of the boy in verse 9 with the response of the disciples who fell away in verse 66?

_____

_____

_____

_____

_____

Faith in Action

God is always present in all our situations. This week, practice recognizing the presence of God by imagining that Christ is physically present with you at all times and acting accordingly.

2. Why do people respond so differently to the word of God? How are you called to respond to Jesus?

_____

_____

_____

_____

_____

Going Deeper

It is one thing to admire Jesus' ability to do miraculous things; it is another to offer to be a part of his miracles. When the boy offered his fish and bread, he was probably offering the meal his family would eat that day. He was taking a huge risk that Jesus could use what he had to offer in a way that would bless his family and so many others who gathered to hear Jesus. As this boy grew up, he probably told and retold this story many times. The offering of his fish and bread would always be associated with the power of this miracle.

> ### Notable Quotable
>
> *"We must be ready to do little things for God; many are willing to do the great things."*
>
> —Dwight L. Moody

Contrast this with the experience of those who followed Jesus across the lake and would not believe that Jesus was sent from God, even as they asked him for another miraculous meal. The crowd chose not to respond with belief to Jesus' declaration that he was "the bread of life" and was offended when he used a Messianic title like "Son of Man" to describe himself. Response to Jesus is easy when it is a free gift, like the meal. It is hard when it will require a person to alter her or his life by following him.

It took a step of faith for the boy to let Jesus borrow his lunch, but with that offering, Jesus multiplied not only the food but the faith of many. Today, Jesus wants us to be a part of what God has planned for this age— the miracle of changed hearts and renewed minds within ourselves and our communities.

Going Deeper Questions

3. Which group do you identify with most: the faithful boy, the questioning disciples, or the people looking for a free lunch? Why?

_____

_____

_____

_____

_____

4. What things in your life are you willing to give up so that God can use them?

_____

_____

_____

_____

_____

Day 2

Today's Scripture

James 2:14-26

Key Verse

For just as the body without the spirit is dead, so also faith without works is dead.

James 2:26 NASB

1. What is the connection between faith and works?

_____

_____

_____

_____

_____

2. In what ways has God called you to serve? When have you listened to that call, and when have you shied away from it?

_____

_____

_____

_____

_____

Going Deeper

Life is full of pop quizzes, moments when we have to respond immediately or we will never have the chance to serve God in that way again. James tells us to keep our eyes open. When we see or hear about the needs of others, that is often the voice of God speaking to us. Knowing when to respond to someone, and when not to respond, requires us to be connected to the Holy Spirit through prayer and worship. One way of doing this is to "practice the presence of Christ," a way of living developed by a monk named Brother Lawrence in the 1600s.

Brother Lawrence was not an educated man when he entered the friary, so he was put to work as a kitchen worker and later a sandal repairer. But instead of being angry about his low position, he believed that every kind of work, no matter how small, could be used as an act of worship that brings us closer to God. When he scrubbed the dishes, he knew that Christ was right there with him, and he chose to work for Christ in whatever little way he could.

> ### Notable Quotable
>
> *"We can do little things for God; I turn the cake that is frying on the pan for love of Him, and that done . . . I prostrate myself in worship before Him, Who has given me grace to work."*
>
> —Brother Lawrence of the Resurrection

Lawrence reveled in just being close to God, and he saw all work, not just Bible study and prayer, as a way of communicating our faith in God. In doing his work, Lawrence was also serving the other members of his monastery. By treating every moment as a chance to serve God, Brother Lawrence was living out James's teaching. He heard God's call in the smallest of things. He blessed others and was blessed with a wonderful relationship with God as a result. You can never miss a chance to serve God if everything you do is a small act of service.

Going Deeper Questions

3. What would you change in your life if you constantly remembered that
   God was present with you?

_____

_____

_____

_____

_____

4. What tasks in your life do you try to avoid? How can you turn these
   tasks into small acts of service to God?

_____

_____

_____

_____

_____

Today's Scripture

1 Samuel 17

Key Verse

David said to Saul, "Let no one's heart fail because of him; your servant will go and fight with this Philistine."

1 Samuel 17:32 NRSV

1. Why would none of the Israelites challenge Goliath? What would happen if Goliath won?

_____

_____

_____

_____

_____

2. Have you ever avoided doing something because you were afraid of failure? What might have been accomplished if you had completed the task?

_____

_____

_____

_____

_____

Going Deeper

The reason that we often do not follow the promptings of God is that we feel overwhelmed by what it will mean if we respond. God sometimes calls us to small things, helping someone change a tire or taking a meal to a neighbor. Other times we sense God prompting us to take on a cause that will require altering our life and changing our priorities and plans.

Goliath of Gath was a big challenger. Real big. He was 9 feet, 9 inches tall, and his armor alone weighed 125 pounds. The tip of his spear weighed 15 pounds, the size of an average watermelon! By contrast, David was probably a young teenager with no experience in fighting a seasoned warrior.

Part of responding to God's callings in life is to recognize that we may look ridiculous to those observing us. David's

> ### Notable Quotable
>
> *"Start by doing what's necessary, then do what's possible, and suddenly you are doing the impossible."*
>
> —St. Francis of Assisi

brothers, or the whole army of Israel, for that matter, must have been convinced that this kid was not thinking clearly when he stepped onto the field with Goliath. God, however, must have been incredibly pleased that David could trust him so deeply and take so great a risk.

Because David's goal was to please the Lord, the Lord blessed David with victory, not only on the field of battle but also as a leader of God's people. The faith of a shepherd boy was the catalyst that saved a nation. Imagine what your faith could do in the world today.

Going Deeper Questions

3. David's family didn't support his actions here. How can we do what is right even when our family or close friends might not support us?

_____

_____

_____

_____

_____

4. What is the biggest spiritual challenge facing your community today? How can you act in faith to help address that situation?

_____

_____

_____

_____

_____

Day 4

Today's Scripture
Psalm 95

Key Verse

Do not harden your hearts as you did at Meribah, as you did that day at Massah in the wilderness.

Psalm 95:8 NIV

1. What is your favorite thing about God's creation? Write a message giving thanks to God for that miracle.

_____

_____

_____

_____

_____

2. Write out two lists—one of things God has blessed you with and one of things God is calling you to do. What do these lists show you about God?

_____

_____

_____

_____

_____

Going Deeper

So often in life, we choose to ignore God's call, whether it is the commandments and teaching of Christ in the Bible or the intuition we gain through prayer. We think we don't have time or it doesn't sound fun or we don't think it will work or we don't know how to do it. When we live independently of God's calling for our lives, we turn our backs on the God who knit us together and gave the whole world shape and purpose. How can we shout "No" to the God who whispered "Let it be" and brought the cosmos into being? When we experience how immense, how powerful, how great God is, it enables us to be humble; and when we are humble before God, we are far more likely to be obedient to God. This was the experience of the psalmist, who calls us to kneel before God as sheep before a shepherd.

> # Notable Quotable
>
> *"If you are what you should be, you will set the whole world on fire."*
> —St. Catherine of Sienna

British Olympian Eric Liddell understood the need to humble himself before God's call. Eric was the son of Scottish missionaries and one of the fastest 100-meter sprint runners in England. His blazing speed earned him a trip to compete in the 1924 Olympics. However, the first 100-meter race was scheduled to run on a Sunday, and Eric steadfastly refused to run on the Sabbath. So he withdrew from the race, and ran instead in the 400-meter race a few days later. Imagine his surprise when Eric won the 400-meter race—and also set a new world record in it!

Throughout his life, Eric continued to follow God's calling, leaving behind his athletic career to serve as a missionary in the poorest parts of China until his death. Eric was faithful in the little callings, and in turn, God gave him a greater calling in life. So no matter how small the call may seem, God can use an obedient follower for great things.

Going Deeper Questions

3. What people do you know who exemplify humility and obedience? What can you learn from their lives and lifestyle?

_____

_____

_____

_____

_____

4. What is something that you've felt led to do, but chose not to? How might you be more obedient to that calling?

_____

_____

_____

_____

_____

Today's Scripture
1 Timothy 4:6-16

Key Verse

Rather train yourself for godliness; for while bodily training is of some value, godliness is of value in every way, as it holds promise for the present life and also for the life to come.

1 Timothy 4:7b-8 ESV

1. How does Paul encourage Timothy to become a better Christian?

_____

_____

_____

_____

_____

2. In what areas of your life do you feel gifted by God? How are you working to strengthen those areas?

_____

_____

_____

_____

_____

Going Deeper

We always have excuses, reasons that we do not respond to what we feel God is asking of us. Our excuses are often a description of our economic situation, our experience level, or our abilities and skills. We have many reasons for the insecurities we share.

Paul tells Timothy that he cannot use age as his excuse because Timothy has all the gifts and abilities necessary to share his faith with others. However, Paul does tell Timothy that to respond to God's calling in his life, he will need to train himself in godliness. He urges Timothy to rely on God, but that doesn't mean that Timothy can just sit back and let God do all the work.

God wants to use us to complete his mission of hope to the world, and the Holy Spirit wants to use everything about us to succeed. That means that the teachings we've received, the Scriptures we've read, our relationships with others, and our conduct in everyday life are all tools that God can use to help touch a hurting world.

> ## Notable Quotable
>
> *"He who governed the world before I was born shall take care of it likewise when I am dead. My part is to improve the present moment."*
>
> —John Wesley

Paul encourages Timothy to continue to grow in knowledge of his faith, and to take what Paul has taught him and pass it on to others. In this way, Timothy would be used by God to bless others by offering them a relationship with Christ. We are also called into that kind of active relationship with Christ, where the Holy Spirit can use all the parts of our lives to bring about God's glory. It's a privilege that God allows us to join in this work—and changes us in the process.

Going Deeper Questions

3. What parts of your life experiences and testimony can God use to help others?

_____

_____

_____

_____

_____

4. In what ways can you continue to grow in Christ so that God can use you more in ministry?

_____

_____

_____

_____

_____

The Decision to Persevere

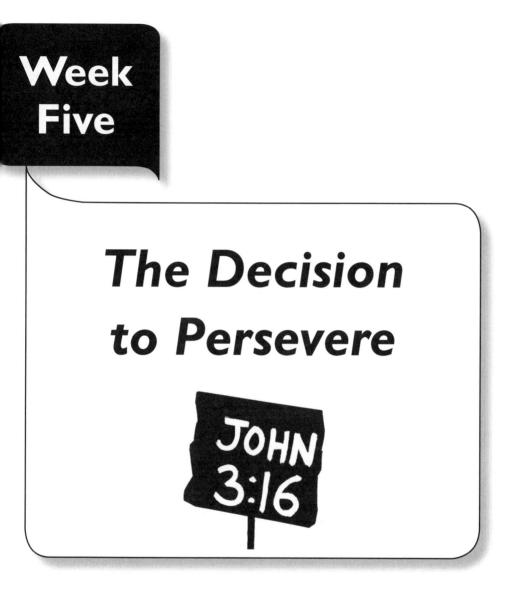

Day 1

Today's Scripture
John 7

Key Verse
Thus the people were divided because of Jesus. Some wanted to seize him, but no one laid a hand on him.

John 7:43-44 NIV

1. Why did Jesus go to the festival secretly?

_____

_____

_____

_____

_____

2. Why didn't the people at the festival understand Jesus when he spoke?

_____

_____

_____

_____

Faith in Action

The world is in need of so much prayer. This week, pray 10 minutes every day for those throughout the world who are persecuted for their faith in Christ.

Going Deeper

Being a disciple of Jesus was about as risky as being Jesus himself. The religious authorities of Judaism found Jesus problematic and even subversive. They wanted him arrested, and his disciples would have been persecuted as well. Perhaps this is why Jesus sends his disciples ahead to attend the Festival of Booths in Jerusalem and does not tell them he plans to attend himself.

In many parts in the world, to follow Christ is to put yourself in a place of great danger. Numerous people still do not want the message of Christ to be shared, and many are persecuted and put to death when they share their faith in Christ with others. Jesus endured such opposition throughout his ministry and was put to death as a result.

During World War II, persecution was especially prevalent, but Christians chose to stand strong in their faith, and many people were brought to Christ by their courageous actions. Corrie ten Boom sheltered many Jews from the Nazis and was sent to a concentration camp for doing so. Dietrich

> ## Notable Quotable
>
> *"In darkness God's truth shines most clear."*
> —Corrie ten Boom

Bonhoeffer preached boldly in Germany, coming back into the country several times after being sent elsewhere. In the end, he was arrested and then hanged just twenty-seven days before the Germans surrendered. St. Maximilian Kolbe was a priest who was sent to Auschwitz. He took the place of a refugee who had been sentenced to death by starvation.

Throughout history, there have been brave Christian men and women who have served the Lord regardless of their situation, and their stories still bring us courage today. Bonhoeffer said that when Jesus called his followers, he called them to "come and die"—that in the death of their selfish desires, they would find new life. This call to sacrifice is one Christians across the globe all have to face in different ways.

Going Deeper Questions

3. What is the most powerful story of Christian sacrifice that you know? What lessons have you learned from it?

_____

_____

_____

_____

_____

4. How are you called to persevere in your own life? What challenges might you face?

_____

_____

_____

_____

_____

Day 2

Today's Scripture
Genesis 39

Key Verse

And though she spoke to Joseph day after day, he refused to go to bed with her or even be with her.

Genesis 39:10 NIV

1. Why wouldn't Joseph give in to Potiphar's wife?

_____

_____

_____

_____

_____

2. If you were punished for doing the right thing, how would you react? How does God tell us we should act?

_____

_____

_____

_____

_____

Going Deeper

One of the hard realities of life is that good people, people who love God, people who are faithful to God, people who are a blessing to others, often suffer. Sometimes they suffer from the injustices of others.

That was the story of Joseph. His brothers sold him into slavery. The wife of his master falsely accused him of sexual assault. No one would have taken the account of a servant like Joseph seriously when a powerful woman like Potiphar's wife leveled such sensational charges. First, Joseph was a slave, then he became a prisoner. An Egyptian prison in the era of the Pharaohs must have been a far cry from the comforts of home Joseph once knew. And yet, by the end of his life, Joseph would be exalted to a position of power and wealth. But during those difficult early years, Joseph had to make a choice—to blame God for his struggles and turn away from his faith or to trust in God's sovereignty and persevere.

> ## Notable Quotable
>
> *"Tribulation [is] a gracious gift of God, a gift that he specially gave his special friends."*
> —St. Thomas More

Enduring suffering is difficult, especially when a person is innocent and treated unjustly. It can lead people to abandon their belief in God. The key to Joseph's faith was his steadfast belief that he was with God, and God was with him. Joseph did not believe that his circumstances were an indicator of God's presence. As a result, he was able to give thanks to God in all circumstances and move beyond every hardship in which he found himself.

Going Deeper Questions

3. What are some reasons God allows people to go through hard times?

_____

_____

_____

_____

_____

4. How do you react when things don't go the way you planned? How should you react, and in what ways can you train yourself to change?

_____

_____

_____

_____

_____

Today's Scripture
Psalm 13

Key Verse

How long must I wrestle with my thoughts and day after day have sorrow in my heart? How long will my enemy triumph over me?

Psalm 13:2 NIV

1. David is obviously in a tough situation and crying out to God for help. Do you feel comfortable calling on God like this? Why or why not?

_____

_____

_____

_____

_____

2. Write down something that is troubling you. Then write a prayer to God both asking for help and praising God for the good things in your life.

_____

_____

_____

_____

_____

Going Deeper

Read this psalm out loud slowly three times. There is something very poignant in this psalm of lament. David shares the difficulty of his present situation in the first two stanzas. The third stanza is quite different. Verse 5 is a reminder of the trust he has had in God in the past and the promise of future joy if he perseveres in his faith. Verse 6 begins with the promise that David will one day sing to the Lord based on the experience of God's past faithfulness.

> ## Notable Quotable
>
> *"Let us not forget: we are a pilgrim church, subject to misunderstanding, to persecution, but a church that walks serene because it bears the force of love."*
> —Archbishop Oscar A. Romero

Memory is a key to perseverance. Recalling how good God has been to us, the people who have been present for us, and the many ways God has blessed us and even rescued us allows us to lose anxiety about the future. When the present is uncertain or difficult, we have to imagine what God can do if we keep making decisions that are faithful to the ways and purposes of God. When we look back to other times in our lives, we can see where God's hand has been present. We can see where the Lord has kept us free from harm or guided our path in a way that strengthened us despite the difficulties we faced.

The psalmist shows that we can be honest with God and still have hope in our salvation. God is not ignorant of our suffering. We may not escape pain altogether, but perhaps we're not meant to. If there were never pain, we wouldn't understand how much we need to trust in the Lord. David understood that trust, and that hope allowed him to rejoice in the Lord's deliverance because he knew help was on the way.

Going Deeper Questions

3. Remember a particularly difficult episode in your life. Looking back, how was God with you through that trial?

_____

_____

_____

_____

_____

4. Do you think that God should deliver us from all trials, or should struggle be an important part of Christian development? Why or why not?

_____

_____

_____

_____

_____

Day 4

Today's Scripture
Daniel 3

Key Verse

If our God whom we serve is able to deliver us from the furnace of blazing fire and out of your hand, O king, let him deliver us.

Daniel 3:17 NRSV

1. Why do you think Nebuchadnezzar set up the gold statue? What was his motivation?

_____

_____

_____

_____

_____

2. What are some of the idols you see most often in the world? What about in your life?

_____

_____

_____

_____

_____

Going Deeper

The world is not well designed for Christian discipleship. Opportunities to worship people and things other than the Lord our God are boundless. Sometimes it is a person asking us to compromise our morals and ethics to bolster their profit margin. Other times, it is marketing that asks us to devote ourselves to the eternal pursuit of cars, homes, and other products.

The three friends in Daniel 3 had to make a decision to persevere. Their fraternal relationship with one another was one of the main reasons they were ready to resist the demands of a king who wanted to be seen as a god. They were willing to die rather than capitulate, and King Nebuchadnezzar gave them that opportunity. Despite multiple chances to save their own lives, Shadrach, Meshach, and Abednego refused to give up their belief in the only God who can save. As a result, when they found themselves in the fiery furnace, they got to have a face-to-face with the God who was their "ever-present help in trouble" (Psalm 46:1 NIV). Their choice to stand for God in a dire situation led not only to their physical salvation but to the spiritual salvation of their captors too.

> ## Notable Quotable
>
> "The greatest proof of Christianity for others is not how far a man can logically analyze his reasons for believing, but how far in practice he will stake his life on his belief."
>
> —T. S. Eliot

In our lives, it is often the case that we can see the presence of God more clearly in the hard times than when things are easy. Sometimes those trials are a way of strengthening our trust in the Lord. But sometimes, the way we deal with our trials can be the turning point for the faith of those around us. God can use all things for his glory, and while "all things" may not always be pleasant for us, it may be just the tool God needs to mold this world into God's Kingdom.

Going Deeper Questions

3. What actions or practices in your life can you change to help others see God's goodness through you?

_____

_____

_____

_____

_____

4. What are some areas of struggle in your life where you are tempted to bow down? In what ways can you continue to fight?

_____

_____

_____

_____

_____

Day 5

Today's Scripture

Acts 4

Key Verse

"Now, Lord, consider their threats and enable your servants to speak your word with great boldness."

Acts 4:29 NIV

1. How did Peter and John respond after they were released? What did they ask from God to help them?

_____

_____

_____

_____

2. In what areas of your life do you feel led to speak or act for Jesus and his teachings? Write a prayer asking for courage and strength in those areas.

_____

_____

_____

_____

_____

Going Deeper

Peter and John were changed men. These once-timid followers of Jesus had become bold men of God. They wanted to tell everyone about Christ and the life they found in him. They were willing to persist in their efforts even if they were arrested. When they were told that they would be freed if they stopped, they did not care. They told the authorities that they could not keep from speaking about Christ.

Richard Wurmbrand knew how that felt. Wurmbrand was a preacher in Romania in the middle of the twentieth century. At the time, Romania was under the Communist control of the Soviet Union, but Richard felt called to preach the good news to the soldiers of the occupying Red Army. As a result, he was arrested and put into solitary confinement for three years.

> ### Notable Quotable
>
> *"Jesus promised his disciples three things — that they would be completely fearless, absurdly happy, and in constant trouble."*
>
> —F. R. Maltby

His cell was underground, and no light was ever allowed to enter. Yet he continued to preach, talking to his fellow prisoners by tapping in Morse code on the walls of his cell. He was eventually released and told that if he went back to preaching, he would be arrested again. Wurmbrand immediately went back to his underground church and did just that. Three years later, he was back in jail, this time serving a twenty-five–year sentence. He was tortured severely for his refusal to denounce his faith. Yet he never ceased preaching. He was later released and became a writer whose testimony and sermons traveled around the world.

Richard, like Peter and John, was a man changed by the passion of Jesus. He would not let his faith be shaken by anything, and he called for Christians everywhere to do the same.

Going Deeper Questions

3. What are some ways persecution still exists in the world and in your area today?

_____

_____

_____

_____

_____

4. Throughout the world today, there are still those being persecuted for sharing their faith. In what ways can you support those Christians and share in their burden?

_____

_____

_____

_____

_____

The Decision to Surrender

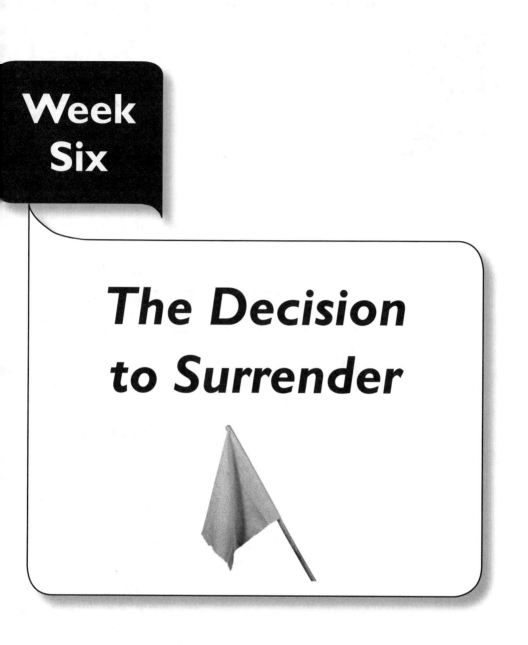

Day 1

Today's Scripture

John 10

Key Verse

My sheep listen to my voice; I know them, and they follow me.

John 10:27 NIV

1. Why does Jesus use sheep to symbolize people?

_____

_____

_____

_____

_____

2. Make a list of ways that God has provided for you like a shepherd for his sheep, and thank God for that deliverance.

_____

_____

_____

_____

_____

Faith in Action

Being in fellowship with God and other believers is key to our Christian growth. This week, attend at least one worship service. If possible, receive Communion at least once at a Wednesday or Sunday service.

Going Deeper

Sheep learn to completely trust their shepherd. They know the whistles and calls their master uses for the flock. They follow their master's signals and gentle prodding. In Palestine the soil is arid, and much of the land is unsuitable for grazing. Water is scarce, and when left to their own devices, sheep often overgraze and destroy the grass in one area before moving on to the next. To top it all off, sheep are easily frightened and prone to wandering. Without a good shepherd, the sheep would quickly die.

> ### Notable Quotable
> *"If I cannot trace His hand, I can always trust His heart."*
> —Charles Spurgeon

The relationship between sheep and shepherd was well known to Jesus' audience. People saw sheep all the time and understood both the limitations of the sheep and the skill of the shepherd in caring for his flock. Jesus invites us to enter into the trust of that relationship, to believe that he works for our good. It is easy to distrust God and believe that the ways of Christ will limit our pleasure rather than enable our joy. But when we understand that the true Shepherd knows better than we do, we can see that the limitations are truly for our benefit. Without guidance, we are prone to wandering into unhealthy relationships and injurious actions where our sinful nature leads us. We can live for our own pleasure and yet damage our lives and the lives of others. Jesus promises to shepherd us away from the pain of this world. All he asks in return is that we listen to his voice and follow where it leads.

Going Deeper Questions

3. How were the Israelites throughout the Bible like sheep? How are we similarly sheepish?

_____

_____

_____

_____

_____

4. The world sees Christianity as just a set of rules. What are some of the limitations that following Christ requires, and how do these "limitations" actually keep us safe?

_____

_____

_____

_____

_____

Today's Scripture

1 Kings 17:8-16

Key Verse

So she proceeded to do according to the word of Elijah. Then the woman, Elijah, and her household ate for many days.

1 Kings 17:15 HCSB

1. How does the widow put her trust in the Lord into action?

_____

_____

_____

_____

_____

2. In what ways do you trust God every day? How can these little acts of surrender build into greater trust over time?

_____

_____

_____

_____

_____

Going Deeper

We cannot trust in someone until we believe they are trustworthy. Elijah received news from God of an upcoming miracle. A widow, during a time of drought and famine, would feed him with an unending supply of meal and oil. It was a fairly moderate miracle. The modest bread she was able to make was not exactly a five-course meal. But it was enough. It was a literal answer to Jesus' later prayer, "Give us this day our *daily* bread . . ."

Elijah trusted God because he had had so many experiences in which responding to God's calling had put him at risk. People in power had tried to kill him. He had to flee to the desert to protect himself. At one point, he was kept alive only by a flock of ravens that dropped scraps of meat to him day after day. Life was hard under normal circumstances, but Elijah's life as a prophet was unusually difficult. Yet whenever Elijah found himself at the end of his abilities and resources, God always showed up.

> ### Notable Quotable
>
> *"Few souls understand what God would accomplish in them if they were to abandon themselves unreservedly to Him and if they were to allow His grace to mold them accordingly."*
> —St. Ignatius of Loyola

Again, we find that memory is one of the key components of faith. When things are going poorly, we often focus all of our attention on our present suffering and forget about the blessings God has already brought about in our lives. But if we can train our memories on God's faithful love, it enables us to recall God's provision in the past, trust that God will provide in the present, and make decisions that allow God to work in our lives in the future. Elijah did not live a life of blind faith; he believed because he remembered what God had done for him, and because of that memory, he brought life-giving faith to all those around him as well.

Going Deeper Questions

3. Why do you think Elijah's life was so difficult? Did this mean that God did not favor him? Why or why not?

_____

_____

_____

_____

_____

4. What situation in your life requires the most trust in God? How has God provided for you in similar situations in the past?

_____

_____

_____

_____

_____

Today's Scripture
Psalm 71; Psalm 121

Key Verse

But I will hope continually, and will praise You yet more and more.

Psalm 71:14 NKJV

1. Name some of the ways that God, the psalmist's "rock" and "fortress," protected Israel in the Bible.

_____

_____

_____

_____

_____

2. Psalm 71:18 speaks of proclaiming God's power to another generation. In what ways do you hope the legacy of your trust in God is passed on to those around you?

_____

_____

_____

_____

_____

Going Deeper

Psalm 71 speaks of God as a rock of refuge and a fortress. There are still fortresses today in the Holy Land. Most of them are the ruins of past strongholds built by kings like Solomon. Some are left over from the time of the Romans or were used during the Crusades. Perhaps the most important one for the Israelites was the fortress of Zion. This fort just outside of Jerusalem was originally a Jebusite stronghold used to defend the city. But during his reign, King David conquered the Jebusites and took the fort—and the city of Jerusalem—as the spiritual home of Israel. There Solomon would build his great Temple to the Lord, and from there, the kings of Israel would rule the nation. The fortress of Mount Zion became a symbol of God's strength and faithful love for those who believed and endured.

> ## Notable Quotable
>
> *"The true follower of Christ will not ask, If I embrace this truth, what will it cost me? Rather, he will say, This is truth, God help me to walk in it, let come what may!"*
>
> —A. W. Tozer

When you see these fortresses today, even though many are little more than shells of the original structures, it is easy to see the confidence that they inspired in those seeking a refuge in times of danger. In the barren terrain in which they are situated, with the region's long history of conflict and warfare, entering a fortress must have been a powerful experience of safety and protection. The psalmist experienced God in the same way. Like the rock outcroppings that provided shade and security, God is immovable. Like a fortress no enemy would dare to attack, God is all powerful. The ability to experience God in such a significant way must have enabled the psalmist to trust God completely and made decisions to follow God easy. In the same way, we can trust God to be our strong tower, an unmoving rock that will stand through our struggles and protect us from the enemy.

Going Deeper Questions

3. The Israelites were constantly surrounded by war. How does their situation compare to our time period, and what can we learn from their belief in God as refuge?

_____

_____

_____

_____

_____

4. From what in your life do you seek refuge? In what ways do you believe God can protect you in your specific situation?

_____

_____

_____

_____

_____

Today's Scripture

Matthew 8:5-13

Key Verse

But the centurion replied, "Lord, I am not worthy to have you come under my roof, but only say the word, and my servant will be healed."

Matthew 8:8 ESV

1. What did the centurion mean when he said, "I too am a man under authority"?

_____

_____

_____

_____

_____

2. Have you ever felt unworthy of God's love and grace? How can we overcome that feeling and trust in the Lord's forgiveness?

_____

_____

_____

_____

_____

Going Deeper

Some people seem to have an incredible trust in Christ that is highly admirable. Often these people come from places that we would never expect. It seems so unlikely that the centurion in this story would have come to Jesus for help, much less believed so deeply in Jesus' power. He was a Roman and not a Jew. He was a soldier who had rank and authority. There were probably few times that he had ever asked an Israelite for assistance. In fact, his fellow soldiers may have thought him weak to ask for anything. Trusting that Jesus could perform a miracle and heal his servant was a whole different level of faith, and trusting that Jesus could do this at a distance, without seeing or touching the man, was unthinkable.

Yet through his trust, this Roman soldier taught the people of Israel—and Christians throughout history—much about the power and love Christ has for people. The centurion possessed two qualities that are important to faith. First, he was a compassionate man. He cared about his servant and apparently appreciated him. He was willing to seek help for his servant and was willing to acknowl-

> ### Notable Quotable
>
> *"Love, to be real, it must cost—it must hurt—it must empty us of self."*
> —Mother Teresa of Calcutta

edge his need to Jesus. Second, he understood authority. He believed that Jesus' power was such that Jesus could simply command the servant to be well, and he would be well. Even Jesus marveled at his trust. Most people in Jesus' life, then as now, spent time asking Jesus to prove himself over and over. How refreshing to see a man who simply trusts that Jesus is sufficient for his need.

Going Deeper Questions

3. Where else could the centurion have turned for help? Why do you think he chose to come to Jesus instead?

_____

_____

_____

_____

_____

4. Who is the most faithful and trusting person in your life? How can you cultivate a similar attitude toward God?

_____

_____

_____

_____

_____

Day 5

Today's Scripture

Revelation 21:1-8; Revelation 22

Key Verse

The one who testifies to these things says, "Surely I am coming soon." Amen. Come, Lord Jesus!

Revelation 22:20 NRSV

1. What excites you most about heaven?

_____

_____

_____

_____

_____

2. How does surrendering our lives to God on earth help to prepare us for eternity?

_____

_____

_____

_____

_____

Going Deeper

Eventually, everything ends. The sermon ends, the service ends, the study ends, the group ends, the Bible ends, and eventually, every human life ends. The revelation John received had a lot to do with the end. Much of this revelation is confusing. Some of it is crystal clear. One author has said that the message of Revelation is, "God Wins."

In these final two chapters, John describes the experience of heaven, where God's reign is not marred by sin or rejected by human decisions. It is a place of utter beauty and abun-

> ### Notable Quotable
>
> *"Trust the past to God's mercy, the present to God's love, and the future to God's providence."*
> —Augustine

dance. It was unlike anything John had ever seen and certainly a world away from the place John occupied in exile when he received this vision. John was on the island of Patmos, and he would have been able to look across the water and see the mainland where people he loved lived while he was being punished for his faith. Imagine the longing he must have felt to be reunited with those he loved. Rather than pictures of his friends and family, God gave him a vision of heaven, knowing that John could trust that all things were in God's hands until the great reunion took place on another distant shore. Decisions he had made for Christ had led him to this difficult circumstance, but still John trusted.

Portions of these chapters of the Revelation of John are often read in hospital rooms to the dying or at funerals to comfort the living. They give us a sense of God's power and the beauty of our destination when our journey with Christ is complete.

Going Deeper Questions

3. God doesn't want us to dwell on "the end," but simply wants us to be ready for it. With that understanding, how are you living with God's future plans in mind?

_____

_____

_____

_____

_____

4. How does John's picture of heaven draw you toward God? How does it impact the decisions you make in your life?

_____

_____

_____

_____

_____

Notes

The following notes offer citations for the Trivia Tidbits found throughout this book. The citations are listed by week and day—for example, "4.1" means the Trivia Tidbit for week 4, day 1.

1.1—Jim Elliott, *The Journals of Jim Elliot* (Grand Rapids, Mich.: Revell, 1978), p. 174.

1.2—Billy Graham, "A Daily Process" devotion, accessed February 16, 2014 (http://billygraham.org/devotion/a-daily-process/).

1.3—Attributed to J. R. Miller. Compare his sermon "Jonah Sent to Ninevah" (1910), accessed February 16, 2014 (http://www.gracegems.org/Miller/jonah_sent_to_nineveh.htm).

1.4—Mother Teresa, paraphrased from *Come Be My Light: The Private Writings of the Saint of Calcutta* (Colorado Springs: Image, 2009), p. 34.

1.5—Thomas Merton, *Seeds of Contemplation* (Norfolk, CT: New Directions, 1949), p. 60.

2.1—C. S. Lewis, *Mere Christianity* (New York: Macmillan, 1952), pp. 198-99.

2.2—Pope John Paul II, "17th World Youth Day—Homily of the Holy Father John Paul II" (2002), accessed February 16, 2014 (http://www.vatican.va/holy_father/john_paul_ii/homilies/2002/documents/hf_jp-ii_hom_20020728_xvii-wyd_en.html).

2.3—Traditionally attributed to St. Agnes, ca. A.D. 300.

2.4—John Newton, quoted in *The Christian Spectator*, vol. 3 (April 1821), p. 186.

2.5—Eugene Peterson, quoted in *The Spiritual Formation of Leaders* by Chuck Miller (Maitland, FL: Xulon Press, 2007), p. 191.

3.1—St. Athanasius, paraphrased from *On the Incarnation of the Word*, Paragraph 54.

3.2—C.H. Spurgeon, "John Ploughman's Talk; or, Plain Advice for Plain People," accessed March 3, 2014 (http://www.spurgeon.org/misc/plowman.htm#Chapter%2014).

3.3—St. Augustine, quoted in the sermon "On the Advantages of Tribulations" by St. Alphonsus Liguori.

3.4—John Wesley, from The Letters of John Wesley. "London, January 1, 1765, " accessed March 3, 2014 (http://wesley.nnu.edu/john-wesley/the-letters-of-john-wesley/wesleys-letters-1765).

3.5—C. S. Lewis, *Mere Christianity*, p. 223.

4.1—D. L. Moody, "The Qualifications for Soul Winning," sermon delivered December 7, 1873, accessed February 17, 2014 (http://www.bible-believers.com/moody_sermons/m1.html).

4.2—Brother Lawrence of the Resurrection, quoted in "The Character of Brother Lawrence" (ca. 1693) in *The Practice of the Presence of God and The Spiritual Maxims* (Mineola, N.Y.: Dover, 2006), p. 61.

4.3—Attributed to St. Francis of Assisi.

4.4—Attributed to St. Catherine of Siena, quoted by Pope John Paul II in an address to the Regnum Christi Movement and the Legionaries of Christ (January 4, 2001).

4.5—John Wesley, Letter to John Smith, Newcastle-upon-Tyne, March 25, 1747.

5.1—Corrie ten Boom, *The Hiding Place* (New York: Bantam Books, 1971), p. 201.

5.2—St. Thomas More, *Dialogue of Comfort Against Tribulation* (1534), Book One, Chapter 20, Paragraph 2.

5.3—Archbishop Oscar A. Romero, *The Violence of Love* (Maryknoll, NY: Orbis Books, 2004), p. 1.

5.4—T. S. Eliot, quoted in *Draper's Book of Quotations for the Christian World* (Wheaton, Ill.: Tyndale House Publishers, 1992).

5.5—F. R. Maltby, quoted in *The Westminster Collection of Christian Quotations*, ed. Martin H. Manser (Louisville, KY: Westminster John Knox Press, 2001).

6.1—Traditionally attributed to Charles Spurgeon.

6.2—Traditionally attributed to St. Ignatius of Loyola.

6.3—A. W. Tozer, "Walking in Truth," accessed February 4, 2014 (http://www.cmalliance.org/devotions/tozer?id=685).

6.4—Mother Teresa of Calcutta, accessed February 17, 2014 (http://www.motherteresa.org/txt/dailyRef.xml).

6.5—Attributed to St. Augustine; source unknown.